AUSCHWITZ

An eyewitness describes how French Jewish children were forced onto trains. About 4,000 of these children died at Auschwitz:

Most of them couldn't even carry their little suitcases ... And the morning of the deportation when we tried to take them downstairs they screamed and kicked ... The gendarmes came upstairs and with a lot of difficulty they made them. One or two of the gendarmes seemed a little bit sad to see this horrible show.

A PLACE IN HISTORY

AUSCHWITZ

SEAN SHEEHAN

WITHDRAWN

ARCTURUS

This edition first published in 2010 by Arcturus Publishing
Distributed by Black Rabbit Books
P.O. Box 3263
Mankato
Minnesota MN 56002

Printed in China

Series concept: Alex Woolf
Editors: Sean Connolly and Alex Woolf
Designer: Phipps Design
Picture research: Alex Woolf

Library of Congress Cataloging-in-Publication Data

Sheehan, Sean, 1951-
  Auschwitz / by Sean Sheehan.
    p. cm. -- (A place in history)
  Includes bibliographical references and index.
  ISBN 978-1-84837-672-4 (library binding)
  1. Auschwitz (Concentration camp)--Juvenile literature. 2.
Holocaust, Jewish (1939-1945)--Juvenile literature. 3. Jews--
Persecutions--Europe--Juvenile literature. I. Title.
  D805.5.A96S54 2011
  940.53'1853858--dc22
          2010014147

Picture credits:
Arcturus: 16 (LMS).
Corbis: cover *background* (Bettmann), 6–7 (Sygma), 11 (Bettmann), 14 (Arnd
Wiegmann/ Reuters), 15 (Bettmann), 17 (Wiener Library/epa), 19 (dpa), 20
(Bettmann), 22 (Frank Leonhardt/epa), 23 (Michael St Maur Sheil), 25 (Carmen
Redondo), 26 (Michael St Maur Sheil), 28 (David Sutherland), 30 (Bettmann), 35
(dpa), 36 (Benjamin Lowy), 37 (dpa), 40 (Auschwitz Museum/Reuters), 41
(Auschwitz Museum/Reuters), 43 (Michael St Maur Sheil).
Getty Images: cover *foreground* (Galerie Bilderwelt/Hulton Archive),
8 (New York Times Co/Hulton Archive), 9 (Hulton Archive), 12 (Galerie
Bilderwelt/Hulton Archive), 13 (Hulton Archive), 18 (Galerie Bilderwelt/Hulton
Archive), 21 (Galerie Bilderwelt/Hulton Archive), 24 (Imagno/Hulton Archive),
27 (Galerie Bilderwelt/Hulton Archive), 29 (Julian Herbert), 31 (Roger Viollet),
32 (Hulton Archive), 33 (Galerie Bilderwelt/Hulton Archive), 38 (Galerie
Bilderwelt/Hulton Archive), 39 (Janek Skarzynski/AFP).

Cover pictures:
Foreground: Jewish children, survivors of Auschwitz.
Background: The entrance to Auschwitz-Birkenau concentration camp.

Every attempt has been made to clear copyright. Should there be any
inadvertent omission, please apply to the publisher for rectification.

SL001438US   Supplier 03 Date 0510

I am completely normal. Even while I was carrying out the task of extermination I led a normal family life ... From our entire training the thought of refusing an order just didn't enter one's head, regardless of what kind of an order it was ... I guess you cannot understand our world. I naturally had to obey orders.

Rudolf Hoess, camp commandant at Auschwitz

CONTENTS

1. DESTINATION AUSCHWITZ

On March 27, 1942, a train departed from Drancy, just north of Paris, for a place called Auschwitz in Poland. It was not an ordinary train and nor were its passengers. The train was the first to carry people from France to a Nazi death camp. In all, some 65,000 people, mainly French Jews, would be taken on trains to Auschwitz; most of them would be gassed to death there.

The first people to depart from Drancy were Jewish refugees who had fled from eastern Europe, hoping to find safety in France. They were fleeing from a Nazi Germany that regarded Jews as not worthy of life. Germany had conquered France in 1940 and a special French force had been established to round up all Jews in the country. They were then held at a detention camp at Drancy until transport to Auschwitz could be arranged.

The first train continued on to Compiègne, about 60 miles (100 kilometers) northeast of Paris, where a further 558 French Jewish men were marched onto the train. Arriving at Auschwitz, the men were driven into barracks in the newly built death camp. Unlike their wives and children, who over the coming months would be gassed within hours of reaching Auschwitz, the men were worked to death as slave labor. All but a few were dead within five months.

Later, trains arrived pulling cattle trucks packed with Jewish men, women, and children, including the sick, the elderly, and babies. They were forced together, often with no food, water, or toilet facilities, and with barely enough air for the two-day journey that ended at Auschwitz.

Nearly 13,000 Jews, including more than 4,000 children, were rounded up in and around Paris over two days in July 1942, and sent to Auschwitz. Some of the children are pictured here.

2 THE ROAD TO AUSCHWITZ

More than a million people were killed at the Auschwitz death camp. Auschwitz was the largest of a network of death camps situated in Nazi-occupied Poland between 1942 and 1945. Altogether it is estimated that six million Jews were murdered in these camps and elsewhere— around two-thirds of all the Jews in Europe. This systematic attempt to exterminate an entire people is known as the Holocaust.

Rise of the Nazis

The road to Auschwitz and the Holocaust began a quarter century earlier in Germany in 1918. After World War I (1914–18), Germany's economy was very weak and

Nazi troops hold anti-Semitic placards in front of a locked storefront during a boycott of German Jewish businesses in Berlin, Germany. One of the signs reads: "Germans Defend Yourselves! Don't buy from the Jews!"

many Germans felt humiliated by their country's defeat. Political parties offered different solutions. Right-wing groups, growing in popularity, blamed Jews for Germany's troubles, offering people a scapegoat. Anti-Semitism, a prejudice against Jews, was common across Europe at that time. In 1919 a young anti-Semite named Adolf Hitler joined a small right-wing group, the German Workers' Party. By 1921 he was its leader and the group had become the Nazi Party.

By 1933, in a parliament where no single party had a clear majority to rule the country, Hitler had built up enough support to be offered the job of Chancellor. Hitler used his position to pass a law that gave him the powers of a dictator. The Nazi Party was now in control of Germany and could pass whatever laws it wished.

Anti-Semitic laws

In 1933 all Jewish civil servants lost their jobs and there were public burnings of books written by Jews. The following year saw Jewish actors and musicians banned from performing and Jewish law students were barred from taking their exams. More anti-Semitic laws were passed and in 1935 Jews lost their German citizenship.

Large prisons, called concentration camps, were built to incarcerate anyone who opposed the Nazis. Citizens were arrested, sent to the camps without a trial and lost their rights. It became dangerous to say or do anything that was not supportive of the Nazi government.

Smoke pours from a Berlin synagogue after it was set on fire by a Nazi mob during the Kristallnacht riots of November 9, 1938.

FACT FILE

Anti-Semitism: 1938

March Germany annexes Austria: 180,000 Jews lose their citizenship and jobs.

September Germany annexes Sudetenland in western Czechoslovakia. Tens of thousands more Jews lose their rights.

October 15,000 ethnically Polish Jews are deported from Germany into Poland.

November 9 Known as Kristallnacht, or "night of the broken glass": hundreds of Jewish synagogues are burned and Jewish shops attacked in an organized act of violence by Nazis. Jews are murdered and 20,000 are sent to concentration camps in Germany.

German expansion

Under Hitler, Germany built up its armed forces and became, once again, a powerful country. Hitler's plan was to expand German territory, firstly by annexing land where there was a German-speaking population (Austria and the Sudetenland), and then by conquering neighboring Poland.

By 1939 Germany's Jews had lost their citizenship and their rights. No other country had done anything to try to stop the persecution of the Jews, although many countries had allowed some Jewish refugees in. Some Jewish citizens from Austria and Czechoslovakia were able to flee to other European countries, but many more became trapped when their countries came under Nazi control.

On September 1, 1939, Hitler invaded Poland. Two days later, Britain and France declared war on Germany. This marked the start of World War II, a conflict that would last for the next six years and spread right across the globe.

Einsatzgruppen

The conquest of Poland brought two million Jews under Nazi control. Before the war, the Nazis had been content to confiscate the possessions of Jews and drive them out of Germany. Now, under cover of war, the Nazis were able to take more extreme measures in the knowledge that their actions were unlikely to be discovered. Their goal was the complete destruction of Jewish life and culture in Europe. To this end, a policy of persecution soon developed into one of mass murder.

Special murder squads were created, called *Einsatzgruppen*. They followed the German army as it advanced through Poland. When they arrived at a town or village, the *Einsatzgruppen* rounded up the Jews for execution. Usually they shot them and buried them in mass graves.

FACT FILE

German conquests 1938–41

September 1938 Germany occupies Sudetenland in Czechoslovakia.

September 1939 Germany invades Poland.

April 1940 Germany invades Norway.

May 1940 Denmark, the Netherlands, and Belgium conquered by Germany.

June 1940 France is invaded and defeated by Germany.

June 1941 Germany invades the Soviet Union.

German soldiers march through a street in Poland following the German invasion. The Polish capital, Warsaw, was captured before the end of September 1939.

Ghettos

Many thousands were killed by the *Einsatzgruppen*, but the number of Polish Jews was so great that the Nazi leadership decided that a more efficient method of dealing with them had to be found. Special areas of Polish cities were created, called ghettos, to contain Jews until it was decided what to do with them. At first, life in a Polish ghetto was hard but tolerable. It became worse as more and more Jewish people were forced to live there, and food and other essentials became increasingly scarce.

Invasion of the Soviet Union

The Soviet Union was a vast country made up of Russia and many other smaller states. Hitler was determined to conquer the Soviet Union to provide *Lebensraum* (living space) for the German people and to control its rich natural resources—especially oil. Germany invaded the Soviet Union in June 1941, and the *Einsatzgruppen* once again followed behind the army and set about its task of murdering Jews.

By the spring of 1942 as many as a million Jews in eastern Europe and the western Soviet Union had been killed and buried in

The Warsaw Ghetto became the largest Jewish ghetto in Europe, with an estimated population of 400,000. As conditions worsened there, people were reduced to begging.

FACT FILE

Number of Jews under Nazi control in 1941 (approximate)

Baltic countries	253,000
Belgium	65,000
Belorussia	375,000
Bulgaria	64,000
Denmark	8,000
Finland	2,000
France	350,000
Germany/Austria	240,000
Greece	70,000
Hungary	650,000
Italy	40,000
Luxembourg	5,000
The Netherlands	140,000
Norway	1,800
Poland	2,000,000
Romania	600,000
Russia	975,000
Slovakia	90,000
Ukraine	1,500,000
Yugoslavia	43,000
TOTAL	**7,471,800**

Source: *The War Against the Jews 1933–45* by Lucy S. Dawidowicz (Penguin, 1987)

mass graves. New ghettoes were also created to provide accommodations for Jews who were used in factories and in the fields as slave labor.

In the Babi Yar Massacre of September 1941, nearly 34,000 Jews from Kiev in the Soviet Union werc massacred by the *Einsatzgruppen*. Here, SS officers are about to execute some of the Jews before pushing their bodies into a ditch.

The Final Solution

Back in Germany, experiments had already been carried out to develop ways of killing unwanted people such as prisoners of war and the mentally handicapped. Nazi leaders came to view poison gas as the most efficient way of killing people. This method, they decided, could be used for killing Jews in very large numbers.

Some time in the second half of 1941 a decision was made to murder the entire population of Jews in Europe. The Nazis called their plan the "Final Solution to the Jewish Question." No records exist of who decided this, or how the decision was arrived at or when the decision was made, but the person chosen to organize and oversee the genocide was high-ranking Nazi Heinrich Himmler.

VOICES

Witness to a massacre

Herman Graebe, manager of a German construction firm in Ukraine, witnessed Jews being forced into a large grave:

They lay down in front of the dead or injured people; some caressed those who were still alive and spoke to them in a low voice. Then I heard a series of shots. I looked into the pit and saw that the bodies were twitching or the heads lying already motionless on top of the bodies that lay before them.

3. PREPARING FOR AUSCHWITZ

By early 1942, with millions of Jewish people under their control, the Nazis had begun to plan, build, and put into operation six death camps where Jews could be murdered in much larger numbers than was previously possible. The largest of these camps was Auschwitz. As well as being a death camp, it was also a complex of factories where Jews the Nazis deemed able could be used as slave labor.

The Wannsee Conference

In January 1942, leading Nazis met at a villa in Wannsee, a suburb of Berlin, to be told of the plan for dealing with Europe's 9.5 million Jews. The Jews would be rounded up from all areas of occupied Europe and North Africa and then sent to camps in Poland. There they would be worked to death. The minutes of the meeting do not mention murder but say that those who survived the work would be "treated accordingly" to prevent "a new Jewish revival." From this statement the true intentions of the Nazis to murder all Jews was made clear.

The villa at Wannsee, where senior Nazis met on January 20, 1942, to agree plans for the Holocaust.

Heinrich Himmler (1900–45) became the head of the Nazi SS in 1929 and Germany's minister of the interior in 1943.

A list of the number of Jews in each country was distributed and the rules about who qualified as a Jew were clarified. They agreed that German and Austrian Jews should be deported first so that Germans made homeless by Allied bombing could take over Jewish housing.

Death and work camps

Auschwitz was just one of a vast network of prison camps built by the Nazis. During the war the camp-building program accelerated.

Hundreds of small camps were built, mostly using Jewish slave labor. Following the Wannsee Conference, some of these camps were designated as death camps. The first of these was Majdanek in Poland. Originally built to hold Soviet prisoners of war, Majdanek was attached to a munitions factory and later became a sorting center for property taken from those gassed in other camps.

This map shows the location of the six death camps in Poland, as well as some of the more important Nazi concentration camps.

Auschwitz, the German name for the Polish town of Oswiecim, was established in 1940 as a prisoner-of-war labor camp. The planners of the Final Solution soon came to view it as an ideal location for their purposes. Auschwitz had good train connections to other parts of Europe and this made it especially suitable as the location for both a death and a work camp.

It would be easy to bring in fresh supplies of slave labor, and the rail connections also made it convenient for the distribution of goods made in the camp's factories. Auschwitz grew to become the largest of the death camps, as well as a center of industrial activity.

Four more death camps—Chelmno, Belzec, Sobibor, and Treblinka—were built. Like Majdanek and Auschwitz, they were built in occupied Poland, in locations with good transportation connections but away from the public gaze. These four, however, were built purely as extermination centers—deportees were usually killed on arrival. The only people not immediately killed were those needed to dispose of the corpses. Around a third of the six million Jews murdered under the Nazis died at these four camps. More Jews, however, went to Auschwitz than any other camp, and it was there that the largest number of Jews were murdered.

Deportations

Hitler's war against the Jews had begun on a relatively small scale with the *Einsatzgruppen* In late 1941 and early 1942, a new stage began. With the building of the death camps and the transportation of thousands of Jews to these camps from the ghettos, the Holocaust had developed into a massive administrative undertaking.

The first large-scale deportations began in December 1941 when victims were sent by train to Chelmno. In March 1942, one of the first transports of Jews arrived at Auschwitz. These were mostly Polish Jewish refugees who had reached France only to be later rounded up and deported.

As the Holocaust gathered pace, the ghettos began to empty, and the Nazis devoted more resources to rounding up Jews who had until then evaded their attention. Deportations occurred very regularly. A Jewish girl, age 12 in 1942, remembered how "people were being taken away every day and at that time we did not know where they were being taken to."

A view of the gate tower and train line at Auschwitz in Poland. More Jews were murdered here than at any of the other Nazi death camps.

VOICES

What will I get in return?

Lucille Eichengreen recalls arriving at the ghetto of Lodz:

We had to sleep on the floor of a classroom. And once a day we would get soup and a little piece of bread. When I tried to get my sister into the hat factory [those who worked were given better rations] it was impossible …the answers I got … [were] "What will I get in return?" In the ghetto everything was paid for one way or another.

Jewish councils

Trains were filled with Jews taken from different ghettos. They were either selected by the Jewish councils that ran the ghettos or randomly taken from their homes or off the street. The Jewish councils carried out work that served the interests of those organizing the Holocaust. They maintained a police force within the ghettos and drew up registers of all the Jews living in the ghettos. From these registers, the Jewish councils made up the lists that determined who would leave for a death camp on a particular day. Members of the Jewish councils had little choice but to do this work. However, they undoubtedly helped the Nazis implement the Holocaust. For this reason, they have been severely criticized by some Jewish historians.

Death camps

The trains took Jews to the nearest death camp. Unless they were sent to Auschwitz or Majdanek, where they might find themselves placed in a work camp, few deportees survived more than 24 hours beyond their arrival.

At Auschwitz, Majdanek, Belzec, Sobibor, and Treblinka, new arrivals were sent into chambers disguised as shower units where

In 1941, Jewish men are transported from the Warsaw Ghetto to work on sites elsewhere in Poland. The following year, the same men would be sent to Treblinka to be murdered.

Hungarian Jews arrive at Auschwitz early in 1945. Up to three trains left Hungary for Auschwitz each day over a period of 50 days. The chimneys of the crematoriums can be seen in the background.

they were killed with poison gas. Their bodies were then burned in crematoriums or on outdoor pyres. At Chelmno, a different procedure took place. Jews, mostly from neighboring Polish towns, were brought by train to a nearby halting place and forced into large vans. While the vans were driven toward crematoriums, the Jews inside were gassed by the exhaust fumes of the engine.

All six death camps were managed by a special Nazi force called the SS. Each camp was managed by about 30 members of the SS, each of whom was a high-ranking officer specially selected for this task. The SS group managing each camp was supported by a body of guards who were usually either men who had previously been part of an *Einsatzgruppen* squad or were local people recruited for the task.

FACT FILE

The SS

The SS—standing for *Schutzstaffel* ("protection squads")—was originally created as a squadron of bodyguards for high-ranking Nazis. Under Heinrich Himmler's command, the SS grew into an enormous force of nearly a million men, working both as frontline soldiers and political police. Unlike regular soldiers and police, the SS were ultra-loyal to the Nazi cause and had a reputation for ruthlessness. The work and death camps were placed under SS authority. At Auschwitz, the SS functioned as overseers because the camp had evolved a system where discipline was maintained by inmates, known as *kapos*. A court system in the SS maintained discipline among the troops and some SS soldiers were actually convicted of brutality and sent to prison.

4 A SMALL PLACE IN POLAND

In the spring of 1940 Auschwitz was just a collection of derelict army barracks outside the Polish town of Oswiecim. It was chosen as a suitable site for a concentration camp to hold Polish political prisoners. An SS officer named Rudolf Hoess was appointed commandant of the camp in May 1940. Hoess and his family lived in a house screened off from the rest of the camp. He ordered 30 German convicted criminals to be sent there to guard the prisoners. The first prisoners arrived in June 1940 and were used as laborers to turn the site into a concentration camp.

Rudolf Hoess, the commandant of Auschwitz, boasted at his postwar trial that he ran "the greatest extermination center of all time."

VOICES

Building the camp

Wilhelm Brasse, who later became the camp photographer, recalls the early days of building:

We used very primitive tools. The prisoners had to carry stones ... I worked at demolishing houses that used to belong to Polish families. There was an order to take building materials such as bricks, planks, and all kinds of other wood. We were surprised the Germans wanted to build so rapidly and they did not have the material.

Slave labor

Even in its very early days, Auschwitz was seen as a potentially profitable enterprise that could contribute to the Nazi economy through the use of its prisoners as slave labor. This started on a small scale, using prisoners to work in nearby sand and gravel pits, but grew much larger when a major German company, I. G. Farben, decided to build a factory only a short distance away. Rudolf Hoess began offering camp inmates as workers in the I. G. Farben factory in early 1941. By 1944 the factory was making use of 83,000 slave laborers.

Experiments with gas

One of I. G. Farben's companies produced a pesticide called Zyklon B, a poison gas that was used at Auschwitz to kill rats. It was the camp's deputy commandant, Karl Fritsch, who had the idea of trying it out on people.

The first experiments were carried out in September 1941. A group of Soviet prisoners of war and sick Polish prisoners were locked in an airtight cellar. Zyklon B pellets were dropped into the room through vents, releasing the poison gas. Within 20 minutes all the prisoners were dead.

The growth of Auschwitz

Heinrich Himmler first visited Auschwitz early in 1941 and he made it clear that the place would play a central role in his plans for the Final Solution. In stages, Auschwitz began to change and increase in size. The original camp, known as Auschwitz 1, became the site's administrative center.

Heinrich Himmler (second left) carries out an inspection during the construction of Auschwitz III–Monowitz in July 1942. The officer on the right is Rudolf Hoess, commandant of Auschwitz.

VOICES

Testimony by Hoess

In his autobiography, written in prison after the war, Rudolf Hoess expressed relief that a method of killing other than by shooting had been developed:

I must admit that the gassing process had a calming effect on me. I always had a horror of the shootings, thinking of the number of the people, the women, the children. I was relieved that we were all to be spared these bloodbaths.

In October 1941 a new camp was built, known as Auschwitz II–Birkenau. Birkenau was a nearby village, which was cleared of its inhabitants. The site's first inmates were 10,000 Soviet prisoners of war who were used as slave labor to build the camp's barracks. These Soviet prisoners were the first to have numbers tattooed onto them, a form of identification that would later be extended to the Jews arriving at Auschwitz. Auschwitz II–Birkenau (often shortened to "Birkenau") would become the extermination camp.

Auschwitz expanded again in 1942, when a third camp, Auschwitz III–Monowitz, was built to hold the people who were sent to work at the nearby I. G. Farben factory. I. G. Farben was the largest of the industrial enterprises at the Auschwitz complex, but it was by no means the only one. Prisoners were also sent to work at two local coal mines, and around 50 smaller camps housed slave laborers who worked in a cement factory, a steel factory, a shoe factory, and a plant for defusing unexploded bombs. At its busiest, Auschwitz had 7,000 guards and about 150,000 slave laborers.

FACT FILE

Birkenau

As well as gas chambers and crematoriums, Birkenau contained a disembarkation point for arriving cattle trucks carrying Jews, a women's camp where women selected for work were housed, and a gypsy camp where Roma families were kept. About 90 percent of the people who perished at Auschwitz during World War II died in Birkenau. Most were Jewish but the victims also included Polish non-Jews, Roma, Jehovah's Witnesses, homosexuals, and Soviet prisoners of war.

The main gate at Auschwitz with its sign "Arbeit Macht Frei" (work sets you free), erected in June 1940. The sign was stolen in December 2009, but was recovered soon afterward by the Polish police.

Replicas of the ovens at the Auschwitz crematoriums.
After removal from the gas chambers, the bodies
were burned in these ovens. Tall chimneys were built
above the crematoriums to carry away the smoke.

The killing factory

In early 1942 two cottages at Birkenau
had their insides bricked up, making them
airtight. Known as the Little Red House
and the Little White House, they were the
first gas chambers at Auschwitz. At first
the dead bodies from these gas chambers
were taken to a crematorium in Auschwitz I
for incineration. As the rate of killings
increased in late 1942 and early 1943, new
gas chambers and crematoriums were
constructed within one building for greater
efficiency. By the summer of 1943, four of
these gas chambers/crematoriums were in
operation. Auschwitz had become a killing
factory, where murder could be carried out
on an unprecedented scale.

FACT FILE

Ordinary Germans and Auschwitz

Germans knew that the Jews had been
sent to special camps, and public auctions
were held to dispose of confiscated Jewish
property. However, it is difficult to be sure
how much ordinary Germans knew about
the true nature of what was happening at
Auschwitz and the other camps. The many
SS soldiers who worked in the camps
wrote letters home to their families and it
is probable that some information would
have leaked out. After the war, most
Germans claimed ignorance of the
Holocaust; some, though, would almost
certainly have heard rumors.

5 HOW AUSCHWITZ WORKED

Jewish people arrived at Auschwitz by train, day and night. When they disembarked, everything appeared calm and well organized. The deportees had been told they would be found accommodations and work and had been instructed to bring with them a suitcase of personal belongings. On arrival, their luggage was taken away by men wearing the striped uniform of camp inmates. SS guards formed men and teenage boys into one line and women, girls, and younger children into another.

The selection process at Auschwitz: within minutes of arrival people were selected either for work or death. The men and women are wearing the yellow stars that identified them as Jews.

VOICES

I'm not going to see you no more

Everything went so fast: left, right, right, left. Men separated from women ...The sick, the disabled were handled like packs of garbage. They were thrown in a side together with broken suitcases, with boxes. My mother ran over to me and grabbed me by the shoulders, and she told me "Leibele, I'm not going to see you no more. Take care of your brother."

Leo Schneiderman, Auschwitz survivor

The selection process

SS doctors inspected the lines, telling each person to go either to the left or the right. Those sent to the right were regarded as fit enough to work in the slave labor camps. The others were led away to the gas chambers. They included women with babies, children, the elderly, and the sick. SS officers explained they were to take a shower and undergo delousing. The victims were led into a changing room and told to undress before walking into the gas chamber. Usually these people were dead within two hours of getting off the train.

Everything about the extermination facility was made to seem as normal as possible so as not to panic the victims.

The gas chambers were disguised to look like shower rooms, complete with dummy shower heads. The Zyklon B was even transported to the gas chambers in a vehicle made to look like an ambulance and marked with a red cross.

Those considered fit for work—typically about ten percent of the trainload—were sent to the barracks, thinking they would be able to see their families later. They were told to take off their clothes and hand in their valuables. They were given a tattoo of their camp number, had their hair shaved off, received a uniform, and were then driven to the work camp.

The remains of one of the gas chambers at Birkenau. The Nazis tried to destroy the evidence of their crimes when they knew that defeat was certain.

FACT FILE

Arrivals

The Auschwitz–Birkenau State Museum estimates the numbers of captives arriving at Auschwitz between 1941 and 1944 as follows:

Jews

1941:	1,000
1942:	197,000
1943:	270,000
1944:	600,000

Non-Jews

1942: 1500 Poles; 10,000 Soviet prisoners of war.

1942–44: 160,000 Poles, Roma, Byelorussians, Ukranians, French, and others were recorded. About 10,000 more prisoners were never recorded as having been there.

The work camps

The daily routine in the work camps was intended to work underfed and sick people to their deaths. The day began at 4:30 a.m. with a roll call. Everyone—even those who had died in the night—were lined up and counted, a process that could take hours. Those prisoners who looked too sick to work were taken off to the hospital or to the gas chambers.

After roll call, people were given various duties. Some were given jobs in the kitchens or the hospital or in "Canada"—the sheds where the clothes and possessions of the most recent victims were sorted. These people could steal food or other valuables and use them to trade for a blanket or give them to their friends.

Different jobs

Carpenters, electricians, sewing machinists, and doctors might have an easier life if chosen to carry out their trade in the camps.

VOICES

Canada

Working in Canada saved my life because we had food, we got water, and we could take a shower there … We always managed to smuggle clothes … we gave away all those clothes because we didn't need them … we ate the food. It was a rescue for us … We wanted to live. We wanted to survive. To have food, water, and enough sleep—those were the things we cared about.

Linda Breder, Auschwitz survivor

Inmates at Auschwitz slept in three-tiered wooden bunks in large barrack rooms, each housing between 500 and 1,000 prisoners. They retired here at the end of each day to receive their rations of bread and water.

Slave laborers at work in Auschwitz in 1942. Prisoners often died from starvation or exhaustion within a few months.

A few women were given administrative jobs. Others were not so lucky and were sent to build roads, new buildings, or to the quarries or coal mines. They rarely survived for long. Some inmates were given the job of *kapo*, or overseer. Knowing one of the *kapos* was an advantage because they could be bribed to hand out easier jobs. The *kapos* received privileges, including better rations, and were more likely to survive.

At the end of each day's work, inmates were marched back to their barracks, given soup and bread, and taken in groups to the latrines. The few hours of sleep, locked up in stuffy or freezing huts, crammed together on bare wooden bunks, was the only break from the routine of work.

VOICES

I. G. Farben

Norbert Wollheim's job was unloading heavy material from trains needed at the I. G. Farben factory:

Prisoners who broke down were beaten by the German I. G. [I. G. Farben] foreman as well as by the kapos *until they either resumed their work or were left there dead. I saw such cases myself.*

The diet for workers at the I. G. Farben factory amounted to only 1,100–1,200 calories a day (equivalent to about two candy bars), leading to a weight loss of around 7 pounds (3.2 kilograms) each week for an individual. After about three months, most people were too weak for work and were sent to the gas chambers at Birkenau.

6 DEATH AT AUSCHWITZ

During the time that Auschwitz operated, around 1.1 million people died there. They came from almost every country in Europe. The gas chambers built to facilitate their murder were efficient killing machines. The gruesome task of dealing with the dead bodies was carried out by selected Jews who were forced to carry out SS orders or be killed themselves.

In an area at Auschwitz that once housed a gas chamber, a small shrine stands in memory of what took place there.

VOICES

Deceived into death

They were told to undress and the SS said to them: "Remember well the number of your clothes-hanger, tie your shoes together properly, put your clothes into one heap so that you may receive everything on the other side ... There is coffee waiting for you in the camp"... After they were naked they had to walk forward on the left side towards the gas chambers.

Yehuda Bakon, a *Sonderkommando*

The gas chambers

Believing they were about to take a shower, the victims undressed in an outer chamber. They were then divided by sex and sent down the passage that led to the gas chamber. Once the chamber was full, the doors were shut and Zyklon B pellets were poured through vents in the ceiling by a man wearing a gas mask. When exposed to the air, the pellets released deadly cyanide gas. According to Rudolf Hoess, it took about ten minutes for everyone to die. The chamber was then ventilated with fans before the bodies were dragged out by Jewish camp inmates known as the *Sonderkommando* (German for "special unit").

The crematoriums

The dead bodies were hosed down by the *Sonderkommando* before being hauled to an elevator. This took the bodies up to ovens in the crematorium, built on the ground floor, above the gas chambers. At the height of the murders in 1944, 20,000 people were gassed and cremated each day. The crematoriums were unable to deal with the vast numbers of corpses and many were destroyed in huge fires in open pits. The ashes were then dumped in nearby rivers or ponds, used for landfill, or sent to farms to be strewn in the fields as fertilizer.

Much of the evidence of what went on at Birkenau comes from *Sonderkommando* Jews, some of whom wrote down what they witnessed. They placed their letters in containers, which they buried in the ground close to the crematoriums. One wrote: "Dear finder of these notes, I have one request of you . . . that my days of Hell, that my hopeless tomorrow will find a purpose in the future."

These empty cannisters of Zyklon B were discovered by the Russian soldiers who liberated Auschwitz in 1945.

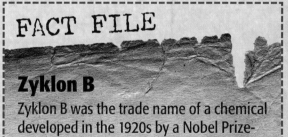

FACT FILE

Zyklon B

Zyklon B was the trade name of a chemical developed in the 1920s by a Nobel Prize-winning Jewish chemist, Dr. Walter Heerdt, for use as an insecticide. It consisted of hydrogen cyanide and a stabilizer in the form of small pellets. It was delivered sealed in small cans that, when opened and exposed to the air at a temperature above 78 degrees Fahrenheit, converted into a lethal gas.

FACT FILE

Josef Mengele

Dr. Josef Mengele was one of the SS doctors at Auschwitz who decided which of the new arrivals could work and who would die. He also conducted medical experiments on inmates, often without anesthetics, and took a particular interest in twins. He collected about 3,000 sets of twins, most of whom were murdered and their bodies dissected for his experiments. Twenty-six sets of these twins survived the Holocaust.

Josef Mengele, a medical officer at Auschwitz, was known for his well-dressed appearance. He would indicate with a flick of his finger which prisoners should live or die.

The *Sonderkommando*

The *Sonderkommando* were useful to the camp authorities because they spared members of the SS from having to carry out the most gruesome duties of the death factory. Most aspects of the process, from escorting victims to the gas chambers to the burning of corpses and disposal of ashes, were handled by *Sonderkommando* Jews, with only a handful of SS men supervising. One of the few tasks they were not given was handling the cannisters of Zyklon B, and its release into the gas chambers.

Jews were selected for *Sonderkommando* duties on their arrival at Auschwitz, before they even knew about the gas chambers. They could not refuse to carry out this work. Their only other option was to commit suicide.

One *Sonderkommando* unit met the trains and took away the luggage of those arriving. Another unit escorted the condemned to the gas chambers, reassuring them along the way that everything would be fine.

After a gassing, the bodies would be removed by another *Sonderkommando* unit. Before the bodies were put in the ovens, the *Sonderkommando* would sort through their clothing, selecting what was worth keeping. Any gold teeth were removed, the long hair of women was cut off (for making into cloth), and bodies were searched for any hidden valuables—the Nazis were intent on making whatever profit they could from their murderous activities (see page 36).

The usual SS practice was to kill the *Sonderkommando* after a few months and replace them with newer inmates. However, Auschwitz became so busy that a few *Sonderkommando* kept their duties long enough to survive the war.

VOICES

A Sonderkommando barber

Morris Venzia, a Greek Jew, was selected for the *Sonderkommando* when the Germans asked for someone with experience as a barber. He was given the job of cutting off the hair of the dead and was there when the chamber doors were opened. He recalled:

I see them all standing up, some black and blue from the gas … women with children in their hands.

Special privileges

The *Sonderkommando* had a more comfortable existence than prisoners in the work camps. They received better rations and were also able to keep any valuables they found on victims' clothing. They could trade these with corrupt SS men for extra food, alcohol, and cigarettes. The *Sonderkommando* slept in separate barracks from work camp prisoners. This was to prevent the prisoners from finding out what had happened to the Jews who had been separated and led away from them after disembarking from the trains.

A collection of shoes taken from the victims at Auschwitz. Any items of value were sorted and stored before being sent to Germany.

VOICES

Leaving for Auschwitz

Alice Lok Cahana, a 15-year-old Hungarian Jew, worked in a factory owned by her family until the Nazis arrived. The factory was then sold to a man named Krüger for one dollar. Alice walked under guard to the train station from where she departed with her family to Auschwitz:

And here was Mr. Krüger watching us go by, not with compassion but with glee—the owner of our factory, the owner of our house. And at the same moment our dog jumped up and recognized us and started to bark.

The killing increases

In 1944, the remaining 60,000–70,000 Jews in the Polish ghetto of Lodz were put on trains to Auschwitz. This was the last of the Polish ghettos to be emptied of its inhabitants, and by this time there were few Jews remaining in western Europe. Nevertheless, in 1944 the rate of killing at Auschwitz increased and the camp became the site of the largest mass murder in world history.

That year saw the completion of a new train line at Auschwitz. Until then, trains had arrived at Auschwitz I, the original camp, and the selection process took place there. Now

May 1944: Jews deported from Hungary disembark from a boxcar onto the crowded station platform at Auschwitz.

a short train line was added, splitting off from the main line and running direct to Birkenau. Victims now disembarked onto a ramp that was only a 100 yards away from two of the crematoriums. Hoess also ordered the digging of five new pits for the burning of bodies taken from the gas chambers. The number of *Sonderkommando* was increased from 200 to nearly 900.

Auschwitz was now equipped to deal with its victims more efficiently than ever before. The camp was ready to receive arrivals from Hungary, and the killing process reached a new level of intensity. Hungary was an ally of Germany, but had not until that time surrendered its Jewish population of more than half a million. This changed in 1944 when the Nazis invaded and took control of the country. Over the course of nine weeks, nearly half a million Hungarian Jews arrived at Auschwitz and most of them were murdered. The killing of the Hungarian Jews over those few weeks accounts for almost half of all the murders at Auschwitz.

FACT FILE

The Channel Islands

Germany occupied the Channel Islands, a part of Great Britain, in 1940. Shortly afterward, without any protests, the island authorities followed German orders to isolate the few Jews who had not already fled. It is thought that three Jewish women from Guernsey died in Auschwitz after the British police ordered them to report for deportation in 1942. Others were sent to detention centers in France and survived the war.

These Hungarian Jewish men were selected for forced labor shortly after their arrival at Auschwitz. Between May 2 and July 9, 1944, more than 430,000 Hungarian Jews were deported to Auschwitz.

7 LIFE AT AUSCHWITZ

Those who were selected for work in Auschwitz became parts in a machine designed to provide maximum profits for German business. Beyond that, their lives were worthless. Any attempt to escape or any sign of weakness was punished by death.

The system of slave labor at Auschwitz deliberately aimed to destroy any sense of hope or individuality among its workers. They could be beaten for any reason by the *kapos* who ran the daily routines. The workers' only hope was to survive another day. Some lost even lost the will to do that and became like walking skeletons, near to death, unable to look after themselves and seemingly unconcerned as to whether they lived or died.

Resistance

The harsh conditions were designed to prevent any thoughts of escape or disobedience, yet there are a few recorded acts of resistance. There may have been many more—most witnesses to what went on at Auschwitz never lived to tell their story.

In June 1944 a woman named Mala Zimetbaum and a man, Edward Galinski, escaped from the camp dressed in a Nazi uniform and civilian clothes. They were captured, and Galinski was hanged while Zimetbaum committed suicide. In 1944 four women were hanged for supplying explosives from the munitions factory to members of the *Sonderkommando*. The *Sonderkommando*, believing they were about to be gassed, blew up one of the crematoriums and set fire to another one. They cut through the fence and escaped. Within hours, most of them were hunted down and shot.

Another act of defiance occurred when a woman refused the order of an SS officer, threw her shoe in his face, seized his revolver, and shot him. Other women began to attack SS officers at the entrance to the gas chamber, severely injuring two of them. The SS men fled and returned with machine guns. One by one the women were removed from the gas chamber building and shot.

VOICES

Making a decision

Pelagia Lewinska chose how she would conduct herself in Auschwitz:

They wished to destroy our human dignity ... to fill us with horror and contempt toward ourselves and our fellows ... And if I did die in Auschwitz, it would be as a human being. I would hold on to my dignity. I was not going to become the contemptible disgusting brute my enemy wished me to be.

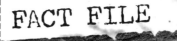

Escaping from Auschwitz

It was extremely difficult to escape from Auschwitz because there were regular roll calls, and if anyone was missing the SS searched the area with specially trained dogs. There was also a terrible price to be paid because if anyone escaped, ten prisoners, selected from the block where the escapee had lived, were starved to death as a punishment.

Part of the barbed wire fence surrounding Auschwitz. Security was very tight at the camp. Nevertheless, around 700 prisoners tried to escape, of which about 300 were successful.

A profitable enterprise

Auschwitz was intended not only to be an extermination center but also a source of profit for the German state. All the property of the victims was collected and sent back to Germany. The clothes were given out to German citizens, the women's hair was used to make cloth, uniforms, paint brushes, and insulation material, and the gold and money helped pay for the war effort.

Part of the collection of human hair that was found at Auschwitz after the camp was liberated. Every woman had her head shaved shortly after arrival at the camp.

VOICES

Everyone knew

A British prisoner of war at Auschwitz, Charles Coward, said:

The population at Auschwitz was fully aware that people were being gassed and burned ...They complained about the stench of burning bodies. Of course all the Farben people knew what was going on. Nobody could live at Auschwitz and work in the plant, or even come down to the plant, without knowing what was common knowledge to everybody.

Georg von Schnitzler, the former head of sales at I. G. Farben, pleads "not guilty" at the war crimes trials in Nuremberg, Germany, in 1947. He was sentenced to five years in prison.

The companies that owned the factories at Auschwitz paid for the use of the slave labor that the camp made available to them. They paid around 3 to 4 marks (75 cents to a dollar) per slave per day, while the cost of upkeep for a prisoner at Auschwitz was about 1.3 marks per day. It has been estimated that Auschwitz made a profit of up to two million marks per month. Over its four years of operation, it made approximately 60 million marks profit.

I. G. Farben

Of the more than 50 German companies that made use of the slave labor at Auschwitz, the largest was I. G. Farben. To maximize its profits, the company treated its workers as a commodity and gave them the least amount of food possible to keep them alive and working. When the workers were too weak to carry on, they were taken to the gas chamber and replaced by others. The company also used prisoners to test some of their products. In developing treatments for typhoid, for example, prisoners were deliberately infected with the disease. After the war, the men who ran I. G. Farben claimed that they had not known about the gas chambers. However, it is known that they made visits to the camp and an I. G. Farben-owned company manufactured the Zyklon B used in the gas chambers.

8 THE END OF AUSCHWITZ

By the summer of 1944, as Soviet troops fought their way across the shattered towns and countryside of eastern Europe, the Nazis realized that it was only a matter of time before they would reach Auschwitz. The SS began to evacuate prisoners, taking them back to Germany to industrial plants where they could still be used as slave labor.

A photograph, taken shortly after the liberation of Auschwitz in January 1945, showing some of the female slave laborers in their barracks.

VOICES

Leaving Auschwitz

Ibi Mann was a prisoner in Auschwitz:

They gathered us in the middle of the night and we never knew the time, the hour, nothing ... If anyone even dared to bend down to get muddy snow off their shoes they were shot; that was the end ... On both sides of the roads there were ditches, big ditches and the ditches were full of bodies.

The ruins of a gas chamber-crematorium at Auschwitz. Many of the camp buildings were destroyed by SS officers in an unsuccessful attempt to conceal their crimes.

Closing down the camp

From September to November 1944, most of the *Sonderkommando* were murdered. One of the crematoriums was dismantled in November and the other three were blown up in December. The last use of a gas chamber was in November 1944. After that, SS officers burned as much paperwork as they could in order to leave no evidence of their part in the Holocaust.

By mid-January 1945 only about 60,000 people remained in Auschwitz, still working each day in the camp's factories. Soviet troops were expected any day now, and the SS decided to leave, together with all the prisoners still able to walk. It was winter, and the prisoners selected for departure wore thin camp uniforms. They had little or no food or shelter at night. Thousands died of exposure or were murdered on what became known as death marches. Those who survived reached overcrowded concentration camps in Germany, and here many more died from illness or starvation.

FACT FILE

Death march

One group of 3,000 people left Birkenau on January 18, 1945. They walked on foot and then rode in open cattle trucks for more than 300 miles (480 kilometers) into Czechoslovakia. Hundreds were killed at a town called Mikolai. By January 21, when they passed through a town called Ratibor, there were just 1,500 still alive. They finally finished their journey three months later. Only 280 people survived.

Liberation

More than 7,000 prisoners remained at Auschwitz when the SS left. The departing SS troops left behind a few guards to keep order in the camp. While they awaited the arrival of Soviet troops, the guards killed about 700 of the weakest prisoners. Their plan was to kill the remaining prisoners, but as Soviet troops neared the camp, the guards fled.

On January 27 Soviet troops walked into Auschwitz. They found hundreds of sick and dying prisoners at the main I. G. Farben factory and the remaining few thousand survivors at Birkenau and the main camp. The Soviet soldiers were battle-hardened veterans who had witnessed human suffering on a huge scale as they advanced westward liberating towns and villages.

Soviet soldiers interview a few of the surviving prisoners at Auschwitz shortly after liberation.

For them, Auschwitz was just another concentration camp deserted by the Germans.

Evidence

The Soviet soldiers found about 600 bodies lying unburied in the camp, heard from the survivors about the gas chambers and found evidence that the SS had not had time to destroy. In storerooms they found 370,000 men's suits, more than 800,000 women's coats and dresses, 40,000 pairs of shoes, and 8.5 tons of human hair. At the time, though, the full horror of Auschwitz was not recognized and little publicity was given to the liberation of the camp.

Survivors start to leave

Field hospitals were set up in the camps, and the prisoners—most too sick to stand—were washed and deloused and given food.

Children who survived Auschwitz display the numbers tattooed on their arms to a Soviet photographer. The Nazis tattooed a serial number onto the arms of all prisoners at the camp to identify and keep a check on their victims.

Hundreds died over the following weeks, too ill to recover despite medical attention from Soviet doctors. Those who did manage to recover gradually regained their strength and made preparations to leave Auschwitz. They either made their own way home or went to special camps for displaced persons in western Europe. Many of those who made it back to where they lived discovered that their homes had been taken over by neighbors and their return was not welcomed.

FACT FILE

The children of Auschwitz

About 700 children survived, most of them because they had been selected for Mengele's experiments and kept in a special building. Of no use back in Germany, they were left behind by the SS. After the camp was liberated, they were sent to displaced persons' camps in western Europe. Most of them were never able to find their families again and lived until adulthood in orphanages.

After Auschwitz

After Auschwitz was liberated, it was used as a prisoner of war camp. The chemical works and other factories were restored to service, and the camp was plundered by local people for bricks and other materials so they could rebuild their homes. Gradually, with the help of survivors and records that had not been destroyed, the true horror of what had happened at Auschwitz began to become public knowledge. In 1947 a section of Auschwitz—the original camp—was opened to the public as a museum and, later, as a research center.

Every year, thousands of people still visit what remains of Auschwitz. Before they fled, the SS soldiers destroyed the gas chambers and crematoriums, so these can no longer be seen. The ones now on show are recreations, based on those found in other camps and on design documents found after the war.

The perpetrators

Himmler, the man in charge of the death camps, including Auschwitz, committed suicide after his arrest in 1945. Trials of other Nazis who bore some of the responsibility for the Holocaust took place after Germany's defeat in World War II. Rudolf Hoess, the camp commandant, and Josef Kramer, his deputy, were both found guilty and executed.

In the 1960s, 21 SS officers who had worked at Auschwitz were put on trial in Germany. Three were acquitted and the others sentenced to terms of imprisonment. In the 1980s and 1990s a few other individuals who had played a part in what happened at Auschwitz were tracked down and put on trial. A far greater number were never arrested or brought to account for what they did. Josef Mengele, for example, evaded capture and escaped to South America, where he died in 1979.

Holocaust denial

A few people, known as Holocaust deniers, believe there was no deliberate mass murder of Jewish people by the Nazi state. Jews died, they claim, from overwork in the concentration camps or as victims of the war. Holocaust deniers maintain this belief despite the great quantity of evidence about what happened at Auschwitz and the other death camps. There are eyewitness accounts of survivors, testimonies from those who worked at the camp, and the records of German companies such as I. G. Farben.

The legacy

Soon there will be no one left alive who was at Auschwitz. But with the help of historians, the evidence of what took place there remains—and it remains for us to think about how it happened and how such a thing can be prevented from ever happening again.

VOICES

Why Auschwitz must be preserved

The Germans did not build Auschwitz to last … [It was] there to serve a purpose: once the Final Solution was solved, these cheap buildings could rot away. Which is precisely why they must be preserved for ever … Immortalizing a building dedicated to wholesale slaughter is the most powerful symbolic rejection of what it stood for. If an earthquake were to swallow it tomorrow, Auschwitz would still have to be rebuilt, brick by second-rate brick.

Ben McIntyre in *The London Times*, January 14, 2010

FACT FILE

The victims

Ninety percent of those who died in Auschwitz were Jewish. They came from the following countries:

Hungary	438,000
Poland	300,000
France	69,114
Netherlands	60,085
Greece	55,000
Czechoslovakia	46,099
Slovakia	26,661
Belgium	24,000
Germany and Austria	23,000
Yugoslavia	10,000
Italy	7,422
TOTAL	**1,059,381**

Non-Jewish victims included:

70,000 Polish political prisoners
20,000 Roma
10,000 Soviet prisoners of war
An unknown number of homosexuals and Jehovah's Witnesses.

Source: www.auschwitz.org.pl

A candle burns on the railroad tracks at Auschwitz II–Birkenau, in memory of those who were transported there by train and never returned.

GLOSSARY

acquittal A judgment that someone is not guilty of a crime.

administration The management of a place.

Allied Describing the Allies, including the United States, Britain, and the Soviet Union, who fought against Germany and the other Axis powers in World War II.

anesthetics Drugs used in surgery that make people unconscious or unable to feel pain.

annex Take over a territory and incorporate it into another country.

anti-Semitism Hatred of Jewish people.

Byelorussian Of or related to Byelorussia, a landlocked country in Eastern Europe, known today as Belarus.

collaborators People who work with the enemy.

commandant An officer in command of an establishment.

commodity Something that can be bought or sold.

crematoriums Places where the bodies of dead people are burned to ashes.

culture The beliefs, customs, and way of life of a people.

denial A refusal to believe that something is the case.

disembarked Got off (a train or boat).

displaced Describing someone who has been forced to leave his or her home or country because of war or persecution.

Einsatzgruppen Special SS units ordered to eliminate enemies of the Nazi state and mainly responsible for the mass killing of Jews and communists in occupied Poland and the Soviet Union.

evade Escape or avoid somebody or something.

extermination Complete destruction of something.

gendarmes The French police.

genocide The deliberate destruction of a racial, religious, political or ethnic group.

ghetto An area of a city where a minority group lives. In the context of the Holocaust, ghettos were areas set aside in some European towns where Nazis forced Jews to live and from where they were deported to the death camps.

gruesome Very unpleasant.

Holocaust The systematic extermination of millions of European Jews and others by the Nazis and their allies during World War II.

kapos Inmates in the Nazi camps who were given the job of keeping order among groups of prisoners.

liberation The act of making someone free.

minutes A written record of what was said at a meeting.

munitions Weapons and ammunition.

Nazi Party The party led by Adolf Hitler that ruled Germany between 1933 and 1945.

overseers People who supervise an operation or a project.

political Relating to politics and government. Political prisoners are people put in prison because of their views about the government.

pyre A heap of combustible material, used for burning corpses.

regime Government.

respite Rest from work or suffering.

right-wing A political term for people who resist change and wish to preserve the status quo.

Roma Short for Romani, an ethnic group living mainly in Europe, who trace their origins to medieval India.

scapegoat A person who is blamed for things going wrong.

Sonderkommando A special group of prisoners who were given tasks within the death camps in return for special privileges.

synthetic Not natural.

veterans People with lots of experience of something.

FURTHER INFORMATION

BOOKS

Auschwitz: The Story of a Nazi Death Camp
by Clive A Lawton (Watts, 2002)

How Did It Happen? The Holocaust
by Sean Sheehan (Watts, 2005)

Surviving the Angel of Death: The Story of a Mengele Twin in Auschwitz by Eva Kor and Rojany Buccieri (Tanglewood Press, 2009)

Surviving Auschwitz: Children of the Shoah
by Milton Nieuwsma (iBooks, 2005)

Timelines: The Holocaust
by Sean Sheehan (Watts, 2007)

Visiting the Past: Auschwitz
by Jane Shuter (Heinemann, 1999)

WEBSITES

www.auschwitz.org.pl/
The website of the Auschwitz museum in Poland

www.pbs.org/auschwitz/
The website of a PBS television series about Auschwitz

www.remember.org
A cyberlibrary dedicated to the Holocaust and the death camps

www.ushmm.org
The website of the United States Holocaust Memorial Museum

INDEX

Page numbers in **bold** refer to pictures.